Carolyn Westbrook

THE FRENCH
INSPIRED HOME

Carolyn Westbrook

THE
FRENCH
INSPIRED
HOME

PHOTOGRAPHY BY
KEITH SCOTT MORTON

CICO BOOKS
LONDON NEW YORK

Published in 2010 by CICO Books
an imprint of Ryland Peters & Small
519 Broadway, 5th Floor, New York NY 10012
20–21 Jockey's Fields, London WC1R 4BW

www.cicobooks.com

10 9 8 7 6 5 4 3 2 1

A CIP catalog record for this book is available from the
Library of Congress and the British Library.

ISBN-13: 978 1 907030 69 7

Printed in China

Photography: Keith Scott Morton
Design: Christine Wood
Copy editor: Helen Ridge

Contents

Introduction

Welcome Home! There is no other place in the world quite like your home. It is uniquely

yours, and it welcomes you with open arms, offering up the sights and smells that are so

familiar to you. While you are away from it, whether traveling around the world or back and

forth on a daily basis, your home waits patiently for your return, like an old familiar love,

to bring life back to it as soon as you walk in the door.

Home is where your family lies about on a comfy sofa, where pillow fights are fought

and won in a bedroom upstairs. It's the familiar creaks of the stair as you climb them or the

sound of a constantly dripping faucet. With all of its imperfections and the infectious beauty

that comes from the people that live there, the laughter and tears that are shared, this is

a place that is loved and worthy of being called home. No matter where your home may be,

you can open it up to a natural time-worn world and introduce the subtle beauty that the

French-inspired interior represents. Soft carvings, gilding, and breathtaking fields of lavender

are just a small part of that beauty.

My first trip to France was life-changing, and I tell anyone who has not been that they

need to see it at least once in their lifetime. The French have an appreciation for detail

that is unsurpassed, along with their appreciation for aged beauty. There are buildings and

structures that have stood for centuries and only grow more valuable and beautiful with

age. Elsewhere in the world, people are often too quick to pull down ancient trees or historic

homes, but in France there is an appreciation of the aged elements that are passed down

through life. Only by realizing the value of time-worn objects is it possible to create a home

with real beauty and tenderness.

You cannot get the look found on the pages of this book by going to a local discount

giant and buying a matching set of disposable surroundings. The classic French-inspired

elements are built for longevity. This is the good stuff that won't fall apart in a few months,

but you have to go out there and hunt it down. The search for anything that appeals to

Right An enchanting vision with all the elements that make for a French inspired home.

you so you can create collections, conglomerations, and collages reflecting your personal interests can begin at any tag sale, flea market, consignment store, or antique mall. You know what they say... one man's trash is another's treasure, and all that. It's true, which can mean great bargains when you're shopping. Plus, you are one step closer to saving the earth as you refresh, renew, and recycle.

Layering is key to the French-inspired look, much like a bird spends endless hours creating its precious nest. All sorts of elements with different textures are brought in, but strength and comfort are, of course, the most vital. The French style is much like my own philosophy: more is better. While I can appreciate modern elements in a room, they must be softened with textiles, such as beautiful curtains, fresh flowers, and soft rugs, or they come across as cold and hard, which certainly does not make for a comfortable home. The French have mastered the art of patterned walls and lush curtains layered with beautiful paintings stacked against and hanging on the wall, and interesting tabletop collections of all sorts of treasures. Gorgeous old, dripping chandeliers set the mood for the perfect French-inspired room, along with rugs that possess the perfect fade from footsteps that have crossed them and from the sun's beams that have shone down on them through the window.

Decorating a home is a sentimental journey, which encompasses objects that were loved and treasured by others long ago and are brought in to be loved and cherished once again. The items chosen will be different for everyone, and that is what makes each of our homes so unique.

On the many occasions that I've walked the streets of Paris, the incredible attention to detail, from the architecture to the golden statues that are just an everyday sight in the middle of the street, was all too apparent. The hand-painted façade of a gourmet shop looked as though it belonged in a museum. The pâtisseries offered their own kind of artwork, with stacks of pastries and goodies piled high on cake plates and displayed to perfection. Storefronts were breathtaking, as were the interiors and the wares on sale. Even the beautiful aqua subway tile designs in the Metro were a stunning work of art. All in all, a sensory overload but in the best possible way.

My search for textiles led me to streets where fabrics were sitting in containers near the curbside for one's approval and, of course, purchase. There were unbelievable toile patterns in all sorts of colors and combinations, waiting to be paired with a silk plaid or stripe. Solid colors of silk were hung side by side, creating the most luxurious stripes. Gathered together in the middle, they would make the most breathtaking curtain you can imagine. This is what welcomed me before I even made it to the brocantes, the French flea markets.

The brocantes are stationed across Paris and are mostly open on weekends. There are magazines available that give the location of the traveling brocantes, which move around to different spots every week. For those of you who love wonderful treasures as much as I do, these flea markets are an incredible experience. There is everything you can hope to find, and then some things that you cannot ever have imagined. I came across beautiful chandeliers, linens, hotel silver, stacks of transferware, and wonderful objects inscribed in French. It's like being a kid in a candy store. Speaking of which, you just have to visit the candy stores, where the candies are displayed in magnificent, huge glass jars, which are decades old. The packaging for some of the candies was also amazing—pastel Jordan almonds came in tiny boxes, pretty enough to be considered jewelry boxes.

Details make a home. Plain and simple. The French, with their amazing attention to detail, can inspire us to create our own work of art in our homes, mixing colors on an ever-changing canvas until we get it just right, for now. Our own homes are to be embraced and enjoyed just as we have created them, reflecting the spirit of those who dwell in them, no matter where in the world. Home is a place like none other. Its delightful eccentricities and inviting smells, not to mention the comfort and familiarity it offers, should make you happy to be in the only place in the world that we call home.

Carolyn Westbrook

Chapter One

A Romance with the French

I remember being with my husband Joe and daughter Alexandria in Paris on Valentine's Day. We strolled along streets lined with fresh tulips, perusing the *brocantes*. Being in Paris on such a day was a dream come true, but my romance with French style had started long ago.

My own style is often described as romantic French, and I do like to add soft, romantic touches to any décor. Layers are crucial in every room. I love decadent layers of fluffy silk curtains, the glorious mix of cabbage roses and hydrangeas in a charming ironstone container... with just the right lighting to create a romantic atmosphere.

Ever since I was a child, I've played house. I was passionate then, as I am now, about creating beauty in a space, no matter how small or simple. I guess that is why one of my greatest pleasures now is making a beautiful space from nothing. I call it creating beauty.

Left This room, which I adore, positively exudes the romantic French style that this book inspires. The gorgeous rug is a work of art. With its huge pink cabbage roses, bows, and swags, it was the inspiration for the room's decoration.

As with any romance, there must be passion, and I am passionate about anything that has been loved and shows its history. When I am shopping, I never really know what I am looking for, only that whatever it is has to speak to me. It's almost as if the object chooses me. I never choose anything based on its monetary value. Many of the oil paintings I buy have holes or rips, but looking at the beautifully portrayed flowers on the old painting used as the backdrop to this tabletop vignette... that is what evokes the romance of collecting, and that's what makes the difference between simply decorating a house and creating a home.

MY LOVE AFFAIR WITH ROMANTIC FRENCH STYLE
IS EVIDENT FROM ALL THE *OBJETS* I'VE COLLECTED
OVER THE YEARS.

My love affair with the romantic French style is evident from all of the *objets* here that I've so painstakingly collected over the years. Like all the loves of my life—and there are many in each part of my home—the French painted desk has been with me for a long time but it keeps evolving according to how I use it in the changing landscape that I call home.

I am often inspired to bring together certain pieces to create a tabletop vignette. The mirrored tray was the inspiration that led me to find the mercury glass vase that was going unnoticed in another room. By placing it on the tray, it becomes a lovely focal point. The pale pink on the vase made me think of a rosebud, so I cut one from the garden. On my way out of the door, I noticed the apothecary jar, almost hidden away in a bathroom, and thought how beautiful it would look filled with pink lemonade. This inspired me to add the goblets, which were tucked away in a buffet, where their beauty was being ignored.

It is so important to keep things fresh. I already had all of the elements that I needed to create this eye-catching vignette but I just needed the inspiration to get it started. By cleaning and moving your collected pieces around, you can create a completely different look for your home. It is always exciting to see something in a whole new way.

Left My romantic French love affair is all too evident in this vignette. A prized Barbola mirror with delicate carvings of faded roses resides next to a hand-painted mercury glass vase with a freshly plucked pastel pink rose, while an aged faded floral oil painting forms the backdrop.

The creamy, faded, and crazed finish on this glass-topped coffee table must be the result of years of service outdoors. In a room that can only be described as French-inspired, the table is a perfect addition. Its delicate, sinuous lines are just the right setting for the cabbage roses and hydrangeas displayed on top in a white ceramic vase. I absolutely fell in love with the color of these flowers. The soft pink and green shades of the hydrangeas change subtly from light to dark, and that is what made them very special to me. Of course, the Staffordshire porcelain poodle was an inspired addition—he was just dainty enough to join this French romance. With the light filtering in gently through the original glass-paned windows and doors, this is a beautiful spot where you simply want to sit and relax and have a conversation, perhaps over afternoon tea.

Right A time-worn outdoor table makes a wonderful coffee table alongside the slipcovered sofa.

This antique painted desk evokes memories of a time when writing letters was an art form, and this is the most perfect writing desk you could imagine. Old family photos on the desk tell a story, as do the letters and notes—in French, they are romantically called *billets doux*. The desk is well outfitted with beautifully detailed desk accoutrements. Everyday stationery items, such as a stapler and tape dispenser, are so ornate that they can be on permanent display in a silver tray, right at hand to make life easier. Multicolored roses in a glass rose bowl seem to mirror the painted roses on the desk. Although flowers may seem like a decadent treat, you can now pick up gorgeous bouquets at the local supermarket. They are affordable for anyone, and just to look at them makes you feel brighter.

Left A hand-painted antique French writing desk is the perfect place to display all of the beautiful accoutrements that make writing letters such a pleasure.

Left From the billowing silk curtains to the carved mirror and elegant dressing table, this room is all about romance.

Above A beautifully detailed silk flower, which once adorned an antique hat, serves as a curtain tieback.

The sound of bustling silk comes to mind as I look at these silk drapes, which are beautiful enough to be French couture. The soft romantic palette with barely a hint of color from the walls is the perfect backdrop. There are many textures here to delight the senses. A silk satin blanket is layered over a monogrammed French sheet, while the bed, piled with down, topped with ruffled box pillows and layers of silk, makes you yearn for a nap. Everyone will enjoy the comfort, beauty, and peace that such a bedroom offers.

Everything in this room seems to work together to create an elegant and stunning look. A glamorous, intimate space has been created between two windows, perfect for applying just the right shade of lipstick or rubbing on a dab of the most treasured *parfum*. The French dressing table exudes femininity, as do the silk drapes , while the sheered silk lampshades and the wonderfully aged urn-style lamps, found at a roadside shop in Alabama, provide the final finishing touches.

My mother has always been my greatest source of inspiration, and I always think of a trip we made to Paris together when I am in this room. We scoured the flea markets and *brocantes*, and she spent an age choosing some glass bottles that she deemed perfect. They are now displayed on the dressing table with some silver containers, which are also hers. Sometimes the right combination of treasures creates a feast for the eyes, with each piece appearing even more beautiful than when displayed alone.

Left A collection of bottles, jars, and containers of all kinds, shapes, and sizes makes an eye-catching statement on an antique silver tray.

Right A corseted chaircover introduces the illusion of couture at a wonderfully ornate dressing table. The dramatic garland swag on the mirror is echoed in the details of the dressing table and bed, making it a defining element in the room.

Left A collection of antique pie-crust mirrors reflects the wonderfully crumbling statue that was once part of a beautiful garden.

Right This is a gorgeous retreat for anyone who loves a good soak in a bubble bath. With perfumed roses, fresh fluffy towels, soft candlelight, and an old-fashioned tub, this room appeals to all the senses, creating the haven of romance that we all crave at the end of the day.

If you could dream up the most romantic bathroom, this might be it. The glowing candles, beautiful bottles and jars filled with scented concoctions, and pastel roses make it the epitome of romance. Some of the roses are just a little bloomed out but, for me, that's when they are at their most perfect and when they smell their sweetest. The soft light filtering through the window is overshadowed only by the twinkling prisms of the French chandelier. Complementing the curvaceous stool, the hat rack is an ingenious way to store damp towels.

This dining room was originally very subdued in style. Everything was white, except for the rug, with its delightful old-fashioned roses. This made me think that I should capitalize on the pretty pink tones of the rug and make more of them. I actually let the rug dictate the overall feel of the room. It inspired the curtains, which are a combination of natural-colored linen and pale pink linen, with French tassel-trim tiebacks in the same colorway. The entire house features one stunning French chandelier after another, and this room was no different. I felt that the dark brown table beneath it was too overwhelming and so softened it with a ruffled, white linen tablecloth.

Left Palest pink and natural tones give this dining room a romantic feel, reminiscent of a vintage valentine.

Squeezed in between the French, slipcovered armchairs is a small, curvaceous table painted in just the right tone of pink for the color palette that I was going for. The romantic look was furthered still more with the addition of Venetian mirrors with pale pink glass, glowing pillar candles, a bountiful assortment of ornamental cabbages and pink roses, and glasses of pink bubbly atop a silver tray. White dining chairs, also from France, surround the table, evoking the French look that is my heart's desire. With colors that remind me of a vintage valentine, the overall effect in this room can only be described as romantic.

Left The pale and dark pink, rose-patterned pillows on the armchairs complement the colors in the rug perfectly, and really seem to tie the room together.

Right An elegant display of ornamental cabbages and roses in various shades of pink makes the perfect centerpiece for the dining table.

All the elements that make for a comfortable and soothing space are present in this French-inspired room, where you can easily imagine curling up with a good book as you revel in its splendor and sophistication. The antique cherub statue is dripping in pearl couture, while the white plumes alongside the pillar candles make their own unique arrangement and add to the overall softness. Soothing tones of pale green feature throughout—in the crocheted throw draped on the ottoman, the throw pillows, and the architectural pieces. An aged floral oil painting in soft greens and pinks hangs from a vintage peeling shutter.

As you look closer, you can really appreciate the French influences of this impromptu collection. The battered French books are remarkable in themselves, but as they sit atop the Florentine table next to the antique cherub, you can really see how something very simple can make quite a statement. Books are a great decorating tool, and not just on shelves. I like to use them to achieve different heights on a table, piled precariously in an old urn or just tossed about almost randomly. French books are, of course, the most desirable but those with battered good looks are becoming harder to find, and they have quite the price tag these days. I always look for them at garage sales, flea markets, and even recycled book stores.

Right This oversized chair, made even softer with plump, oversized pillows, is designed for relaxation.

Below left Strands of pearls around the neck of a garden cherub and antique books arranged haphazardly on a Florentine table create an uncontrived romantic vision.

Below The intricate beauty of these fading and peeling Madonna statues are reflected in the layered mirrors.

A living room that is meant for living is essential to family life. Slipcovered sofas add to the convenience of this no-worries interior. Echoes of the seaside are everywhere in this room. A huge glass cloche on the coffee table hugs a wooden pedestal topped with a stunning piece of coral, creating a striking focal point. Beautiful silk velvet pillows in aqua complement the turquoise coffee table. The shelves are laden with antique French shell art boxes, which I happen to collect and adore. Stacks of fabulous books, comfy chairs with soft throws, and a completely soothing neutral palette remind us of our continued love affair with a seaside-inspired home. The collection of antique mercury glass on the mantel dates way back and is truly impressive. Helping to warm up the room is a sea grass rug. Put together, all these different elements create a look that is totally inspiring.

Left The relaxed style that this room represents, with slipcovered sofas, dreamy pillows, and fabulous treasures from the sea, is one that we all would like to achieve.

The white armchair is the anchor for this corner of the room. The chocolate throw, which drapes casually across it, perhaps in anticipation of a chilly night, is a dramatic touch and a look that I embrace. I think a drape on a couch, chair, or bed always enhances a space. They introduce color and texture, and the layering of different textures is essential to the look that I'm after. I feel that a "live" element is also crucial to a room, with flowers and plants bringing an extra little something that makes otherwise dead interiors come alive. The leaded windows, which separate one room from another, are a splendid feature of this little corner, as are the magnificent stacks of vintage white books and old ledgers. Although it looks rather hip and modern, the dome-shaped chandelier is actually a vintage piece. Garden urns and a table, tall candlesticks, and an antique wire birdcage complete the scene.

Right This little corner adds a wonderful ambience to the entire room.

Below The large glass garden dome, or cloche, looks magnificent over this piece of coral. The entire room brings together the color, beauty, and romance of the sea.

These images encapsulate for me everything that I adore about the romantic French style. Billowing, lavish draperies, French urns and chairs, crystal, and silver are just the start. Add to that ornate carvings of garlands, flowers, and silhouettes adorning all kinds of furniture, wall panels, and mirrors, not to mention chandeliers dripping reflective prisms, and you have a timeless, classic romantic room that makes me fall in love with the look time after time.

Garden statuary and ornaments play a prominent role here. A stone cherub wears a glorious French antique, jewel-encrusted crown. On the aqua-painted coffee table, which has just the right age of patina and picks up hints of aqua elsewhere, is a French urn with a white orchid. Another large, crusted urn, also French, adorns the fireplace.

Left A classic French chandelier welcomes visitors inside and lights up the long winding graceful staircase.

Right This crystal beaded work of art with aqua-colored teardrops is capable of making any room look special.

First impressions count, which means that the decoration of the entrance to a home is very important. It needs to greet and welcome guests, and also make them feel at ease. This entrance is especially welcoming, with its neutral color palette, glorious flowers and vegetation, and beautiful mirrored table piled high with antique mercury glass. The chandelier is massive and spectacular, which it has to be for this enormous space. The gentle curve of the winding staircase contributes to the feminine beauty and sets the tone for the look of the entire house. "Everything French, everything beautiful, and everything pastel" is the mantra touted in this very French-inspired home.

All the chandeliers were imported from France, and they are quite stunning. The old crystal beading and prisms make a grand statement in any interior and cast a light that can only be described as a romantic glow. The delicate aqua teardrops of the small chandelier pick up the turquoise accent color sprinkled around the room, reminding us of the ocean. As they hang from this crystal beaded work of art, they glimmer, making the room appear even more special. I love to add a chandelier to a tiny room and see how its elegance transforms the space—it takes a room to that next level, no matter what its size.

Left This room, used as a den, is awash with white, except for the spectacular splash of pink from the *bombé* chest, and accents of pink dotted here and there.

To the right of the entrance is the front den. It is a confection of fluffy white couches and accents of pastel pink, which could be considered the icing on the cake, while the cherry on top would be the bright pink antique *bombé* chest... *ooh la la!*

Here, and throughout the home, decadently layered silk drapes pool on the floor, and there are plenty of interesting vignettes, including on all of the tabletops. Between the two facing sofas is a wonderful, curvy outdoor metal table, decorated with French-style *objets*. The *bombé* chest is layered with an urn filled with bright pink hydrangeas, while a small silver container holds single roses. Fabulous French mirrors reflect the light of the gorgeous, glistening chandelier. Beneath the chandelier is a tabletop display of a crusted concrete angel draped in antique rosaries. She prays over a loving cup, filled with pink roses from the garden, and a glass cloche with the palest of pink alabaster grapes peeking from underneath.

Left Pale pink alabaster grapes under a glass cloche and a delightful concrete angel create a charming vignette on a glass-topped table.

Right This room is full of the finest French elements: a pink *bombé* chest, an ornate framed mirror, a gorgeous lamp, and the special footstool that was passed down from the homeowner's amazing grandmother, who owned an antique store on Rodeo Drive.

Details, details, details... I cannot stress their importance enough. This house is full of little impromptu collections, put together in a whimsical sort of way but, looked at all together, they are quite fabulous. The tray with pink iced cookies under a glass cloche has been paired with a small scalloped urn containing a delicate green fern, which, in turn, is accented by the bright green limes in a glass bowl. All of these elements come together beautifully. Placed in front of a mirror to reflect the beauty, you have twice the impact.

Another little collection is this basket-style tray, which sits in the kitchen. It offers style and convenience, with the stunning handles of the flatware shown off to perfection and easily accessible. A charming small lamp with a linen shade gives off a soft glow under cabinets, while the tiny shakers provide salt, or *sel*, for cooking.

Below A glass cloche covering pink-iced treats and the lovely green tones of a lacy fern and the cluster of limes create another perfect vignette atop a silver tray.

Left A basket is a good place to house spooners filled with stunning flatware, as well as other dining table paraphernalia and a lamp fitted with a frilled linen shade.

Right These antique carved panels, standing next to a silver tray laden with beautiful pieces of glass and crystal, are typically French.

This is the perfect area for relaxed outdoor entertaining, as well as a glorious retreat. The space is defined with curtains, which can be pulled for privacy, intimacy, or weather conditions. Couches and seating areas are outfitted as any other room in the house, and the ruffled cushion covers in white linen can be whisked off to the laundry whenever necessary. There's even the elegant touch of a French beaded chandelier peeking from the background. Sturdy wicker and curvy feminine metal garden chairs add to the beauty here, while large topiaries and flowers spilling from urns introduce a splash of color.

Below and right The white palette continues to the outdoors and makes for a great place to host an event, with plenty of seating for all.

Chapter Two

The French Country House

A French country house conjures up an image of relaxed comfort—a world of aged fabrics, gold-encrusted mirrors showing their flaking silver, tarnished candlesticks with glowing candles, and threadbare rugs. Some of my favorite French country houses, even though quite sophisticated and with a European flair, have mastered the art of that time-worn, comfortable style. The furniture is sturdy, making it practical for country living, but it is also a feast for the eyes. Aged rugs over plank floors or a leather club chair showing wear in all the right places can transform any room into this favored style of living. The kitchen of a French country house is for those who truly love to cook, and it is functional as well as beautiful. Fresh vegetables are not only colorful but also delicious to eat, showing the more practical side of French country décor. Bedrooms, meanwhile, are layered with sumptuous velvets, velvety roses, and pretty chandeliers.

Left The look of this dining room includes layers of only the best elements, put together in a collage to create the most incredible French-inspired space.

Although the wilderness is never far from the door, inside the French country house there is all the comfort, beauty, and refuge you could need. After leaving behind the fast pace of the city, you can revel in the sights and sounds that only a country house can offer. The French country style is not only practical, but creates surroundings that appear effortless. A table arrangement is put together by just going outside and gathering the necessary items from nature. Long, twisting branches laden with the colors of the season, along with sunflowers that grow abundantly in a nearby field, make for an inspiring work of art.

A FRENCH COUNTRY HOUSE IS
ALL ABOUT SERENITY.

This nature-inspired setting is truly a French inspiration, and although the look is elaborate and stunning, it is neither stuffy nor pretentious. The French chairs, covered in durable cream leather, were a flea market find. Large topiaries, wrapped in burlap and placed in compotes for a different kind of centerpiece, are the "flower arrangement" for the table. Burlap is a favorite of mine, and it makes the ultimate crinkled runner for the time-worn table. Compotes filled with fruit and berries and glass domes covering French herbed cheeses welcome all who dine here. Meanwhile, a bottle of French champagne on a silver tray waits to be poured into the gleaming crystal flutes. On the adjacent buffet, candelabras cast a warm glow alongside the roast turkey and homemade pecan pie, together with a stack of brown transferware plates and all sorts of unpolished antique silver trays, which act as chargers.

As always, it is the details that are important here. My collection of unpolished silver-plated napkin rings, with monogrammed linen napkins folded inside, makes a beautiful addition to the table. Petite votive candles are sprinkled about the table, while small trophy cups, positioned at different heights, add even more interest to an already beautiful tablescape. An antique brown velvet bedspread has become a tablecloth for the round table behind and looks quite elegant as it drapes under the massive flower arrangement.

Right I have always had a love for this enormous mirror. To me, its worn, fragmented silvering is perfect. The reflection is now barely evident and while some would have cast it out for this reason, to me it is the lack of perfect reflection that makes it even more spectacular.

Atop the dining table and buffet, you can see silver hotel serving domes. I collect these and, although difficult to find, they are absolutely wonderful, keeping foods hot and moist until you are ready to serve. I find I use them a great deal during the holidays. The large trophy cup features an interesting collection of concrete mushrooms. I find the whole nature theme very appealing, and there are many examples all around my home. The old French bread basket, lined with a rough piece of natural linen, is a favorite piece—I found it at a French flea market and brought it home in my suitcase. It's ideal for crusty baguettes. Propped up against the antique mirror on the ornate side table is a French etching of the Nativity, together with crystal rose bowls and a trophy cup of flowers. Displaying perfectly the unsurpassed craftsmanship of carving, the table is a true work of art in itself.

Left I am a huge fan of trophy cups. If they're the right shape and have just the right patina, they serve well as vases, candle holders, or planters.

Right The antique mirror reflects the soft glow of the crystal rose bowls illuminated with candles, while the trophy cup is dripping with lovely roses, pheasant feathers, and bittersweet.

On entering the dining room, you are greeted by a marvelous tabletop arrangement of a bountiful bouquet displaying vibrant, colorful stems and autumn leaves, together with sunflowers. The incredible stuffed pheasant, with his natural beauty shining through, is the focus of this compilation. The rugs are aged and a very neutral tone, and so much better than the brand new brightly colored rugs available today. These have a "shine" to them, as they are full of unnatural fibers, unlike their antique counterparts. The old cigar tin depicting a traditional English hunt theme has the perfect faded patina, but what really draws me to it is the way in which its colors mesh so well with all of the other orange, gold, and green tones that you see here.

Another one of my favorite collections is the antique glass spooners on the buffet. I've filled them with all sorts of beautiful and ornate silverware, which I found in Paris at the Porte de Vanves flea market—it was like discovering buried treasure! Stacks of transferware plates on the buffet for guests to serve themselves leave more room on the table. Let us not forget candlelight. It makes the dinner seem much more special and casts a soft, romantic, glow.

Above An extravagant arrangement of flowers and foliage and a stuffed pheasant greet the visitor to the dining room.

Left An ironstone compote filled with fruit makes a wonderful addition to the dining table.

Right Old silver utensils piled inside elegant glass spooners, with silver napkin rings mounded high in an ironstone pedestal compote, make for a very French-style display.

The grayish tones cast by the stone and plaster walls throughout this mansion of a house give the feel of a European castle—it's easy to picture yourself going back centuries and roaming halls lit with glowing lanterns. The lighting, supplied by gas fixtures, is amazing. I am told that there are 105 chandeliers, each one hand-picked in Paris. Two of those are in this boudoir, which is indicative of the French country style.

Wonderful gray tones are evident throughout the room, including in the antique spool bed. The French chairs at the end of the bed are just the right size for sitting in and pulling off your shoes after a hard day. They are upholstered in a neutral toile print, again very French inspired, which gives the room added depth and beauty. The daybed is piled with pillows. Of course, only the finest linen would be the right choice here. Linen is such a great textile because it is natural and has the ability to breathe. The more it is washed, the better it gets, in my opinion. As I have said before... here, in the boudoir, it is all about the layers. You cannot have a proper bed without layering. Silk, linen, down, velvets, and all of the marvelous textures and puffs that make a bedroom a sanctuary—you can find them all here.

The collection of religious art beside the bed is truly stunning. To amass such an assortment of antique pieces takes years of dedication. Each one has been sought after and chosen specifically so that they could all be displayed together and tell a story. The detailing in every single piece is absolutely incredible.

At the opposite end of the bedroom is a sitting area, inside of the large patio. The elegant lines of the chairs make them unmistakably French. Paired up in front of a tall window, these beauties have marvelous views over the water outside. The natural color of the upholstery suits the soothing feel that has been created here, where the water can be heard swishing against the beautiful bedroom patio that extends out over the water, just on the other side of this space.

Above This amazing collection of religious art was amassed over many years, with the express intention of displaying all the pieces together.

Right The bedroom is made all the more beautiful with French furnishings.

Below A pair of French chairs make a cozy seating area at one end of the bedroom.

Left French chairs covered in toile and a large, comfortable, distressed leather sofa offer a great place to relax in true French country house style.

Glorious, layered interiors are a feature of all of the inspirational rooms in this home. The living room has plenty of seating, with a floppy, comfortable leather couch and a pair of wonderful black toile French chairs creating the perfect space for conversation. An enormous ottoman covered in menswear plaid makes for a great table of sorts, hosting a tray of cigar paraphernalia. With just the right amount of crumbling paint, the French daybed is the ultimate place for relaxation, piled high with velvet and toile pillows. A chaise is a beckoning spot to sit and read, while the massive armoire is a charming hiding spot for a big screen television—a beautiful façade for an intrusive feature of modern life. The floors have been polished and glow with the warmth that only wood can offer.

The nature-inspired collection on the covered round table is quite remarkable. It's been achieved from years of poking around flea markets to find just the right elements that will work well together. The natural and neutral shades of burlap form the base of the display, as shown in the tablecloth, antique framed tortoise bookplate, and empty turtle shells. An antique mirror and an architectural piece complete the look.

Below A quirky, nature-inspired collection centered around turtles gives extra personality to the room.

Whenever I am perusing flea markets, whether at home or abroad, I am always on the lookout for aged bookplates. Often featuring insects, animals, fish, vegetation, flowers, herbs, and more, they make the perfect framed collection for any wall in your home. Those from French *herbiers* (collections of dried plants arranged in a book), sometimes dating back to the 18th century, are among my favorites. Many of the bookplates that I find are from the 1920s, which makes me think that hunting for bugs and plants, to be identified, labeled, and placed under glass, was an extremely popular thing to do then. These days, if we are fortunate enough to find such antiques, we can use them as wall art.

The warmth of a pine chest of drawers is the anchor for this side of the room, but the painting is what I consider a work of art. When I am looking for art, its monetary value or whether it is by a well-known artist matters little—the piece simply has to speak to me. The tones of this painting are warm and glorious. The sun is setting in the distance, while the fisherman are beginning to come in from the sea. The urn-style lamps with their dark shades reflect the tones of the black toile chairs. Old leather-bound books add to the warm, rich tones.

Below The beautiful ocean-inspired painting with rich golden tones sets the mood for this sophisticated vignette.

No house would be complete without a fireplace for warmth in winter, and this ornate fireplace doesn't disappoint. But, in summer, it is the oil painting of roses resting on the mantel, layered with antique frames of all shapes and sizes, that is the real eye-catching element. An airy green fern in an old garden urn also makes a fitting decoration.

Layered mirrors, stacked suitcases, and old landscape paintings transform the tiny coat closet. The hat rack is quite ingenious, with old shoe molds serving as hat holders. The attention to detail continues with glass door knobs and a short French chair with a straw seat. It's at the perfect height for removing your boots or shoes.

Outside the closet sits a garden tea cart in a gorgeous shade of peeling green paint. The green is echoed in the collection of water bottles and pile of apples, while the bottom is laden with some magnificent English 19th-century mercury glass apothecary bottles.

My favorite type of home, whether French or not, is one that is not too much of any one style. Even too much "French" becomes a bit boring. The house has to be personalized, and what provides more personality than the wonderful trinkets and treasures that have made your heart pound as you pulled them from the rubble at a flea market? These things were chosen by you, and nothing could represent your home better than your own personal taste.

Left No matter what the season, a fireplace can be beautiful. A magnificent rose oil painting on the mantel, a cherub statue, and a fern-filled urn reside here during the warmer months.

Below An outdoor garden tea cart has been transformed into an indoor cart, holding necessary supplies for the living area, including bottles of water, as well as objects of interest and beauty.

Below right With original inspirational ideas, such as old shoe molds serving as hat pegs, this little coat closet creats enormous impact.

It may be an old saying, but at the heart of every home lies the kitchen. Here, the room is an explosion of purple transferware, which is so difficult to find. Frequent trips to flea markets across the globe have created quite the collection, and it deserves to be the focal point. Lit by old industrial store pendant lights, the magnificent island is a great place to cozy up to and grab a bite to eat. The metal chandelier is perfection over the dark wood table, and is softened by the purple compote filled with flowering narcissus.

This is sure to be one of my favorite kitchens of all time. The absolutely stunning sink, which most of us can only dream of, is set off by the coveted purple transferware platters and Black Forest antlers hanging above. Each cabinet door is hand-made. Behind the arched glass fronts there is even more of that gorgeous purple transferware. Most of us are lucky to find one platter, but here there are at least forty.

Left The heart of any home is always its kitchen.

Right The ideal kitchen should not only be functional but also truly beautiful.

Below One end of the countertop has been given over to a charming vignette of purple hyacinths and wicker-covered bottles.

The collection of purple transferware doesn't stop there. The buffet is crowned with even more pieces of these coveted dishes, from lids to plates to platters. It also hosts a lovely collection of 18th-century bottles and a dark purple spooner filled with sterling flatware.

On the opposite side of the kitchen, looking out on the backyard, there is a warm golden color server next to a fabulous green toile chair. I adore the design and colors of this romantic pastoral scene. The white pitcher decorated with a lavender band is the perfect vessel for the lavender shade of roses, which fit in with the entire color theme here. Compotes of every shape and size house everything from topiaries to fresh nuts to old game pieces. It will come as no surprise to learn that this particular French-inspired kitchen has inspired many others all over the world.

Left While the buffet is definitely English, many of the purple transferware dishes came from France.

Right This elegant chair, covered in green toile, captured my eye, and I happen to love everything about it. The lavender roses alongside match the tranquil lavender theme apparent in all parts of the kitchen.

EVERYTHING IN THIS ROOM
COMES TOGETHER TO CREATE
A DREAMY RETREAT.

This is quite the space to retreat to. A giant French chaise longue angled across the rich wooden floors beckons as you step through the French doors. The chairs in this room are spectacular, covered in a golden hound's-tooth check, with fringed needlepoint pillows introducing feminine sophistication. Old floral paintings, infused with the rich golden tones that inspired this French-style country room, hang on the far wall next to the massive, ornately carved cabinet. A huge coffee table is particularly useful for informal gatherings, as are the layered Florentine tables, which can easily be moved about the room. Stacks of French books, old apothecary jars, and topiaries and plants abound, but the true *pièce de résistance* is the French mirror crowned with a glorious, intricate carving. Positioned behind the chaise, quietly reflecting the room, it is absolutely magnificent.

Left The rich golden tones of this room are typical of a French country house, where comfort and grandeur have equal billing.

A closer look at the coffee table reveals that a prized Barbola mirror has been used as a tray. Stacked on it is a cutting board piled high with rich French cheeses and a crusty baguette. All you need to wash down this simple, typically French repast is a glass or two of a full-bodied Côtes du Rhône. Who would not want to retreat here and be pampered with such luxuries, I ask.

THE TONING DOWN OF THE MASCULINE QUALITIES IN THIS ROOM HAS BEEN MASTERFULLY DONE.

Even the dog is welcome to retreat to this room, which positively exudes comfort and beauty. The balance of masculine and feminine elements here is absolutely perfect. A large, masculine piece of furniture, like this carved wooden cabinet, can so easily dominate a room but that can easily be avoided by balancing it with the layering of soft fabrics, textures, smaller layered furniture, delicate mirrors, and so on. Here, the gentle curve of the legs of the Florentine table is reflected in those of the French chaise, adding softness to all of the wood tones that could overpower the décor.

Left Even the dog is drawn to this room, which succeeds in balancing the masculine and feminine elements to create a space that is truly a retreat.

Below A few lily blooms in a stone vase give height to a well-presented display of French cheeses, a crusty baguette, and a bottle of good red wine.

Sneaking a peek through the archway in this French country home, you can see a decadently layered dining area, lit up by the sunshine as it filters through the stained glass windows. Warm tones are evident here as elsewhere, from the cabinet and tabletop to the upholstered bench. Layers of tablecloths cover the table, which displays a masterful collection of everything from French cheese domes to a gorgeous centerpiece of flowers and greens.

Helping to create a relaxed mood are the luxurious draperies in simple, natural tones. Tucked away in a corner is a chocolate wicker desk, piled high with books. A silver tray of glasses and a pitcher, and a silver trophy cup containing magnolia leaves rest alongside. Casting a welcome glow over it all is a large lamp.

As I've said before, every collection you create should warm your heart. On show among the charming mix of sentimental bits and pieces in the glass-fronted cabinet is an antique watch, worn by a much-loved family member who has passed on. His memory remains, though, in this treasured, time-worn piece.

Left The dining room is a layered mix of all that is warm and inviting, from the glowing candlelight, which casts its magic across the table, to the luxurious drapes. In the background, almost out of sight, is the shadow of the antler rack that holds jackets, throws, and hats. A small table sits below as a place to rest keys and bags as we enter the doorway.

Above right Behind the glass doors of the cabinet is a charming, apparently random, mix of old books, antlers, and other bits and pieces, representing a wonderful conglomeration of memories.

Right A simple chocolate-colored wicker desk, brimming over with books, and a wing chair make a delightful but unexpected reading corner.

These warm-toned wood shelves are to be found on the reverse side of the entrance to the dining room, where they form the centerpiece of the wall. On the top shelf, an enormous silvered punch bowl is used as the planter for a large green ivy, its delicate stems trailing down in front of the wonderful collage of wall art. Among the framed display of old etchings, prints, and chalk drawings—in keeping with the country house theme, these are mainly of animals, specifically dogs—there are yet more of the treasured Black Forest antlers.

Alongside the punch bowl is a fabulous candlestick and many of the items in the home reflect the time that this homeowner spent as an important part of Ralph Lauren Home. We both have a great passion for this style, and who could deny the iconic style that Ralph Lauren represents? All are mesmerized by this homeowner's ability to capture the essence of that. A mixed collection of wicker baskets, and boxes made from wood, basketweave, and pasteboard, makes for attractive storage. They complement the basket that has been turned into a wall ornament, filled with dried hydrangeas. More silver trophy-type vessels look spectacular, along with stacks of interior design books.

Right Flanked by books, boxes, and a trophy cup showing just the right amount of patina, the snowberry branches in a silver urn are an eye-catching feature on the shelves.

Below left Freestanding shelves anchor this wall of the dining room and make a gorgeous statement with the mix of all that is memorable and glorious in an interior.

Below The flowers, stemming from the wonderful French confit, the candles, and the cheese and grapes on the wood chopping board create a welcoming sight. The different elements are so artfully arranged that they resemble a still-life painting.

FOR THE

This room is a quiet masterpiece. All the different elements work together to complement each other. Again, there are warm golden tones, but here they are infused with reds and greens for a richer look. This room represents the beauty of the eclectic mix that I am so fond of. A leather club chair is overlaid with a camel-colored throw and a beautiful rose print pillow. Rugs are layered over one another, and there is a seemingly endless variation of color and textures. There is the softness of a fur throw, and an aged French floral quilt thrown haphazardly under a red and green plaid throw. The ottoman is massive and serves as a coffee table, while the wooden tray on top offers stability for objects placed there. Bowls filled with nuts, a basket brimming with firewood, and a very special painting on the mantel all contribute to the intense beauty of this living area.

Left What a magnificent mix of prints, paisleys, plaids, and floral there is in this truly amazing living space. I would call it a work of art, where you can actually live, read, and relax, and simply be inspired.

Below A simple red and green plaid throw is magically transformed into a thing of beauty when it is the backdrop for the tray with these rich, velvety, red roses. A simple silver dish, filled with warm-colored acorns, also brings out the red of the roses.

Below For me, collections that look as though they just "happened" are always a beautiful thing.

Right In my line of work, I see so much good material that it becomes hard to get very excited over anything except the fabulous, but this particular photo really did excite me, as there is so much beauty encompassed in it.

I absolutely love everything about this corner of the living area. The eclectic combination of the unusual bamboo table with an old mantel clock is a great look in itself. Then you have antique landscape paintings presented in old frames that are as worthy as the paintings they house. An etching of a squirrel is set off beautifully by the old tramp art-style frame. A very ornate silver cup is brimming with the warm, brown tones of pheasant feathers, while the French jar filled with white tulips reminds us of the beauty of spring. A barley twist candlestick sits next to an old box that at one time was used to store someone's treasures. More layers of stacked baskets and the glimmer of a shamrock plant and berries placed in a tiny urn provoke even more interest.

THE LAYERING IN THIS ROOM IS WHAT MAKES IT SO INCREDIBLE.

The all-pervasive red tones are what really work for me in this room and, of course, who could not notice the magnificent dog? Yes, he is quite real and he is really that beautiful and, not to mention, very sweet. As he sits patiently next to the rain boots with their perfect red lining, which somehow brings out the red of the books and all of the plaids, the scene becomes even more appealing.

Although this is a relatively simple part of the room, layers are still used to supreme effect, and that is what makes the room so incredible.

Just off of the living room is this small but incredible French country house-style kitchen. Everything about it feels French, from the floral slipcovered bench in the relaxed dining area to the bistro table, which acts as extra counter space. There is much to take in here with all the layering. A natural linen curtain replaces the door to the laundry, where everything is organized in functional but beautiful baskets. In such a small space, it is essential to utilize every inch. Cooking pots hang from a rack above the stove, and more storage baskets sit on open shelves above with antique wooden cutting boards. A cutting board also serves as a tray over the sink, again offering more counter space. A vintage cabinet is filled with white dishes and brown transferware, which can be grabbed easily for the table. This is plain but practical—its base provides a shelf for baskets of potatoes, table linens, and dish towels.

Left Decorative touches, such as the small prints above the kitchen window, vases and bowls of flowers, and a charming antler hat rack, help to keep the most hardworking room in the house attractive.

Right A short café curtain is a great fit and keeps the focus on the floral linen slipcovered bench, which is such a special part of this room. Even more beautiful seen from this angle, the room captures the heart and soul of what a kitchen should be.

Chapter Three

The French Farmhouse

The French farmhouse... ah, you can just picture it, out
in the countryside, among fields of lavender and large
shady trees, with chickens wandering aimlessly about the
farmyard. But, once inside, you can quickly see that this is
no ordinary farmhouse. Far from it. Many of the farmhouses
featured here are quite sophisticated and, in fact, as
luxurious as they come. A farmhouse is not always about
primitive and rustic. It's a place where large fireplaces
spread warmth across hard wood floors, and massive
exposed beams reveal the sturdiest of structures. It's
where muddy boots are lined up at the back door, and
racks hold jackets and hats that are used outdoors. The
French farmhouse look is relaxed, and stylishness is not
top of its list of priorities, but somehow, such an approach
always seems to result in the best interiors.

Left The library is a personal space, speaking of a love for
fine leather-bound books, history, all things equestrian, and
comfortable, elegant living.

The farmhouse and all of its quaint outbuildings will, over time, become a welcoming site when you return from an outing in the city. To be able to put your hands in the earth and smell the green grass is a refreshing and welcoming change from walking on asphalt.

Of course, decorating this farmhouse is the best of work. The décor can be simple or quite sophisticated, depending on your style. The windows stay up for much of the warmer months as the breeze blows fresh air across the house and into every room. As with any of the different decorating styles covered in this book, collections are always welcomed. There is nothing stale here. This lifestyle is not only comfortable, but appears almost effortless. As you hear the slam of the screen door, you are reminded that there - grown tomatoes just waiting to be picked from the vine... these are the surroundings that beckon you to slow down and enjoy all that life has to offer. Whether time is spent gathering in the garden or gathering with friends for a meal under the stars, this is the way life is meant to be lived... Welcome to the French farmhouse.

Left The lounge area in this farmhouse is filled with comfy couches, chairs, and heavy velvet draperies. It is a gathering space, where much entertaining takes place. Substantial oil paintings and the glow of candelabras add to the convivial atmosphere.

Right A beautifully carved antique mantel adds to the other wonderful elements gathered here, including a fine cigar advertisement dating from the 1800s.

This bar, dating back to the nineteenth century, is quite an incredible find. It is filled with every imaginable sort of liquor or wine, along with wine jugs, crates, and barrels. Wine is served here, and there are many different grape varieties and vintages offered to guests. The impressive cooler, made of solid oak, glass, and mirror, is also from the 1800s and contains everything you could possibly need for a wine or cocktail party.

The bar is the focal point of the many parties that take place at this farmhouse. During those times, this room is busy and the bar counter is laden with all sorts of nuts, olives, cheeses, and, of course, bread. A grand chandelier, completely in keeping with the style of this room, softly gleams overhead.

I noticed a couple of small bottles that not only housed the liquor, but one had a full-sized apple inside, the other a pear. I asked how the fruit got into the bottle, as the opening was quite small. It turns out that the bottle is placed over the blossom and the fruit actually grows inside the bottle until it is ripe. What an amazing process, and well suited to this amazing room.

Right The magnificent old cooler is the focal point of the bar and reflects the masculine beauty of the space.

Left Although massive, this room, with the beautiful strong beams that anchor it and the stone fireplace, has been made cozy and intimate.

Below The shelves are a layered masterpiece, containing small antique landscapes, glorious antique bug collections, stacks of law books, and a lot more. You can gaze at these shelves repeatedly and see something different every time.

Below right This is a truly welcoming scene, complete with comfortable leather club chair and a silver tray laden with decanters, ready to offer visitors a drink.

You really cannot appreciate the awesomeness of this room from these photographs. It is truly massive, and with perfect proportions. Heavy supporting beams contribute a certain sort of rustic charm, while the gigantic stone fireplace offers warmth throughout the house, and a tattered oriental rug layers the floor. Even though the tiger print from the 1800s is far from small, it seems dwarfed by the fireplace. In a room this size there is much shelf space for storing books, works of art, and favored treasures. Here we find a pair of leather club chairs flanking one end of the room, while a surveying tool, set on a tripod and passed down through the generations, is very much in keeping with the atmosphere. Sharing the mantel are peeling concrete lions and an antique trophy collection. The giant French urns are the planters for billowing, lacy, ferns. A multicolored toile covers a pair of parson chairs placed at the other side of this conversation area, while a circular, fringed ottoman provides a serving space. Glowing candles add to the glimmer that the roaring, crackling fire has already set.

This kitchen is beautiful, and in such a home as this one it must be fitted with only the best for the culinary team or chef to whip up the perfect meal for the homeowners.

Against a subway-tiled wall stands a fabulous, gigantic French cabinet. Its shelves are filled with ironstone and silver in the shape of cake plates, pedestals, and plates, as well as magnificent silver serving domes that are used to cover dishes before serving. On the other wall, just out of sight, is the Italian stove, the star of this kitchen, with its $20,000 price tag. An enormous farmhouse sink makes cleanup easy, and there is plenty of preparation space throughout. Fresh herbs, essential for French cooking, are always to hand.

Kitchen essentials—farm eggs, croissants, and fresh milk—sit atop the table ready for the next meal, while wonderful French cheeses abound on the wooden bread board, along with a crunchy baguette.

Chickens are essential to any good French farmhouse home. It's easy to picture the countryside with chickens roaming about and clucking to their companions. Here, all the different-colored chickens, including Araucaunas and Cochins, are mixed together. Between them, they will produce eggs in a range of colors, from pale blue and brown to cream, and all of the shades in between. As well as making wonderful dishes, the eggs also look very appealing, piled in a large bowl on the countertop. These eggs have deep, golden, firm yolks, which are much healthier and essential to French cuisine... well, that and butter, of course.

Left This is a kitchen that is truly meant to inspire cooking, with all of the culinary and serving elements contributing to the décor.

Below Fresh milk and eggs are staples of a French farmhouse.

Bottom Between them, this group of chickens will produce a range of colorful eggs.

This is a very masculine office space, used by a successful businessman who does a great deal of his work here. It is perfect for him as it also represents his various passions, including hunting and history. Although a laptop is usually found sitting next to the ancient typewriter, there is still some magic to be had from the sound of the clackety-clack created by those keys. I still long to see the dark black ink appearing across the page as you press each key.

AN EXTRAORDINARY OFFICE THAT
IS THE PERFECT SPACE IN WHICH TO
GET THE JOB DONE.

As you examine every aspect of the shelves here, you start to appreciate how the haphazardness of their arrangement really works. There are all sorts of flasks, from glass to wicker, and more trophies, with one of the larger ones hosting a twiggy branch and a small nest. The manliness of the display works well, but the introduction of a feminine element in the form of lilies and the lacy, aged bluebonnet landscape paintings creates the perfect, balanced mix.

Left A man's study is not only a place for taking care of business. It should also reflect his style and interests. The bearskin rug and antlers on the wall indicate a passion for hunting.

Top right Photographs that have been passed down capture important events for men of an earlier generation.

Right A closer look at the collected reasures indicate that the room is used by an outdoorsy gentleman.

An old French leather club chair resides elegantly in a hallway between a favored bamboo table and a small chest. The chest is topped with a pedestal and an antique cloche, which houses a perfect, abandoned bird's nest. Aged oil paintings, trophy cups, and, of course, the classic French toile complete this French farmhouse vignette. Straight from a Paris flea market, this is the perfect leather club chair, showing wear in all of the right places. It is this kind of imperfection that helps create the most comfortable interiors.

The pine cabinet in this kitchen provides useful storage for a large collection of cookery books and shows this homeowner's love of food and cooking. Herbs, including rosemary, thyme, and mint, that have been picked from the garden remain fresh in small vases, ready for adding to dishes at just the right moment. A French salt rock can be grated for the freshest and purest salt one can find, and black peppercorns can be crushed using the pestle and mortar.

Left A leather club chair, plucked from the streets of Paris, makes a beautiful statement in any setting, especially when adorned with a toile pillow.

Right A silver tray proves to be useful for these tools of the culinary arts, as the elements are instantly at hand when required.

What could be more dreamy and alluring than these luxurious bedrooms appearing at the end of a hallway? The softness of down and the absence of color make them elegant as well as comfortable. French sconces light one bedroom, while a beautiful chandelier hangs in the other. A glorious night's sleep or perhaps a decadent nap in the middle of the day would be so easy in either of these rooms.

The bedroom is always the first thing to come to mind when you think of soft, romantic spaces. I love the look of the bedroom with the black, antique, scrolled bed and favored white bedding, which shows up so dramatically against it. The absolutely incredible conglomeration of antique oils that flank both sides of the hall leading into this space is breathtaking. The paintings are all different sizes and shapes, with some of them dating back centuries. Some are framed, some are just simple canvases. All of them are truly inspiring.

Left A beautiful, all-white sanctuary beckons from the end of the hallway.

Right The jewels of this hallway are the huge collection of rose paintings. The drama created by the black bed is complemented by the starkness of the white bedding.

For me, this small bath, with the antique, marble-topped chest and fabulous towels layered neatly on the antique towel rack, clearly demonstrates how crucial attention to detail is in creating the perfect home. The hand towels, from all different periods and places, are the work of some very talented women. The hand-made crocheted lace gives them a distinction and makes them unlike any other towel. Brown transferware becomes the artwork in this cozy retreat, along with the wonderful antique rose oil painting that hangs above them. The wall-mounted faucet is a work of art in itself and it is a focal point of the room. This small bath was responsible for me starting to conjure up more ideas for my imagined French farmhouse than I can picture in my mind. It is filled with simple, lovely rooms, like this one, with just the right contents.

Right The perfect French gray painted cabinet becomes even more practical and beautiful as it houses the necessities of the bath.

Below left La Petite sconces add more details along with all the elements that were hand-chosen for this wash room.

Below Again, function and beauty come together for an amazing result.

As we roam through more of my favorite farmhouse retreats, we find this gorgeous bath. This particular one reminds me of those in the old Pontchartrain hotel in New Orleans, only even more elegant. I love the traditional black-and-white floor tiles and the stunning chandelier that illuminates the antique claw-foot tub. Everything about this room was done right in my opinion. The striking mirror is one of the focal points here, and I like the fact that it is just sitting on the floor. Such an elegant piece displayed so casually is very fitting for this room. How marvelous. It is then layered with a smaller dressing mirror and an array of crystal decanters for added interest. Perfect white lilies, snipped from the garden, have been placed in a vase to add even more of a feminine flair to the tabletop. The French charcoal sketches hang in an apparently random fashion and give off quite the feel of the risqué side of French style that they represent. The real focal point here is the awesome black, silk, tufted chair. This magnificent piece of furniture is quite simply a work of art, with its embroidered gorgeous bird that soars across the back... *très magnifique*.

Left The magnificent black French mirror, charcoal sketches, traditional fittings, and black, French, silk-embroidered chair make this a bathroom to retreat to.

Right A small display of glass and crystal housed in a charming glass-front cabinet introduces some shine and beauty to the bathroom.

EVERYTHING ABOUT THIS ROOM HAS BEEN PUT TOGETHER PERFECTLY.

On the rear wall behind the tub is a beautiful black cabinet with leaded glass doors. As you peek inside, you see shelves filled with all sorts of small bottles and decanters that once held cherished French *parfums*, perhaps gifts given by a loved one or treats for oneself, who knows? All of the wonderful smells and feels in this cabinet, from lightly fragranced bubble baths to lotions and bath salts, are displayed beautifully.

The French ambience continues in this living room, which is a favorite for me. I love the mix of the heavy brown beams and harvest table versus the femininity of the rest of the room.

Drapes separate this room from the dining room and bring an additional layer of richness. The dark furniture mixes perfectly with the all-white stone walls, while a fireplace anchors the room. You can imagine spending a night here by the toasty fire during a cold French winter, with the heavy drapes helping to warm the room. Meanwhile, in summer, the windows can be thrown open to let the breezes blow through the house.

The collections on display here, and elsewhere in the house, have been carefully thought out. While shopping in flea markets, you will sometimes come across a spectacular object that you know will be the centerpiece of a collection or arrangement. This is what inspires the whole idea. I am always on the lookout for old books, bottles, old sea shell boxes, and so on. You can never neglect the small things, because it is the details that make the difference.

Left The gorgeous white palette of the living room is richly grounded by the dark beams and fireplace. Slipcovered furniture works throughout the year and makes for easy living.

Right A cleverly placed array of interesting objects, from favored antique shell boxes to pink books and a pink rosary draped around a decanter, have come together for the perfect display.

This could be the ultimate young girl's bedroom. The key to a good bed is layering, and this bed has six layers, including crisply ironed French sheets and antique lace-edged pillow covers. An antique canopy covering is just the thing for this *petit paradis*, and the pure white curtains at the window make the look even more romantic. The painted French desk and the vase of garden hydrangea blooms are just the right faded hue of blue to match the color of the room flawlessly. A huge floor-to-ceiling mirror, carefully propped against the wall, is layered with an antique curved metal patio set, the table covered with a soft, thick quilted cloth and topped with a graceful antique swan planter and swan watercolor painting. This room is fit for a princess, so it's a good thing that one resides here to enjoy all the romance and luxury it offers!

Left A dreamy bedroom fit for a queen or a princess, as the case may be.

Right Too precious to throw away, well-worn ballet shoes that have been outgrown make a pretty display.

This beautifully carved wooden armoire oozes French detail, especially in the antiqued gilding. Such detailing is evident throughout the room, adding to its romantic appeal. The softly layered bed whispers its reflection in the mirror of the armoire and gives us a tiny peek into a world where such luxuries are possible.

Left A dreamy reflection of a dreamy bedroom.

Right A well thought-out collection makes for an interesting corner in this room, with a table skirted in burlap and filled with a collection of mercury glass, old books and statuary, a beautifully arched window pane, and an aged oil painting of hollyhocks.

Chapter Four

French Traditional

As its name suggests, French traditional style is the more established side of French décor but, rest assured, that does not mean boring or stuffy interiors. Although vastly different, all of the rooms featured in this chapter are wonderful spaces, which are a joy to look at. Yet, even though the rooms are so dissimilar, they are all united by those French elements that are a constant reminder of why the French décor is so warm and inviting. The massive, intricately carved mirrors, the chandeliers that cast a magical glow, and the time-worn layered rugs seem to be the common theme in all of these settings. When I think of French traditional, it is these images that come to mind.

Left This is a simple French study in a massive *château*. The French doors let the sun beam into the room, warming the wood floors and creating a very bright and lovely space. This is where the lady of the house works, and the antique print of women is perfect for the pale periwinkle blue walls of her office. Quite the work of art is the century-old statue of St Francis holding Jesus as an infant.

Sturdy wooden gates, a century old, welcome all to this French retreat. As you pass through them, it's like entering another time, another world... one where you can find perfect peace. Large urns, which have withstood decades of weathering, are still quite lovely filled with shrubs and flowers. Newly electrified lanterns light our way and invite us beyond the gate and down the stone path into a different, French-inspired world. Homes like this are places of beauty, where all of your senses are awakened. There are countless delights for the eyes, but also evocative smells, such as perfume wafting from a bubble-filled tub and freshly baked baguettes from the kitchen.

Far left Massive, ancient wooden gates open onto a garden path, which leads around the property.

Left An enormous topiary adds a regal touch to the entrance, while fluffy white cushions soften the setting on this outdoor settee.

The entry to the interior of this French *château* is particularly welcoming. A round table, dressed with a feminine table skirt, is perfect for showing off a wonderful old crusted urn and pedestal, massed with lilies. As guests walk in, they not only enjoy the visual beauty of the arrangement, but also appreciate the faint scent of the flowers. Behind the table are music stands featuring a fine collection of black-and-white photography books. The books are opened at different pages to suit the mood. Displaying books like this is such a brainstorm of an idea and one that I had never seen before. Well done, my friends.

A retreat would not be complete without a warm, inviting library. The hall leading to it is incredible, with floor-to-ceiling mirrors that are layered over with pictures and portraits, ingeniously made possible by a rod-and-chain system. You can see instantly that this is a retreat by the number of rugs that are layered one on top of another, not just for warmth but so that their colors and shapes can be enjoyed as well.

The mirrored wall reflects the room behind, where a finely fringed light fixture spreads light over the grand piano, which is the focus of every party. Literature and music are important in this home. Music stands are used as easels for works of art, and musical instruments and photographs of musicians are everywhere. Family forms the base of this retreat, and the many family portraits create a sense of warmth and caring.

Above left Photographic books displayed on music stands become works of art. The pages are flipped according to whim to create a new masterpiece daily.

Left A luscious bouquet of white lilies welcomes visitors once inside the door.

Right A mirrored hallway is expertly designed with art and photographs layered over the mirror and suspended from chains. An arched doorway allows an enticing glimpse into the library, while the mirror reflects the opposite room in the background.

Once inside the library, you can really appreciate what a magnificent space it is and with so many welcoming elements. There are stacks of books—something for everyone to enjoy, seated in one of the cozy chairs. A good reading light, positioned here next to one of the chairs, is essential. Men and women alike can retire to this library after dinner for a little cognac, even a cigar.

The tabletop is an interesting collage of nature, beauty, and literature. An enormous trophy cup is used as a vase for the rich red spiraling roses, which bring out the few color tones that are present here. Alongside, a dark carved candlestick hosts a red candle. An antique piece of taxidermy is displayed on an antique pedestal, while a glass dome covers a pile of small antique books that feature short stories from previous masters of the written word. The shelves are filled with old, leather-bound classics.

What would the world be like without books? Some people talk of books becoming obsolete as the computer age grows but, for others, the written word, the smell of a book, running your hand across a page that was written decades ago, still holds a certain appeal, which a computer screen cannot come close to offering. There are times when you need to be able to hold onto something and see the dark printed words on crisp paper.

Left Accents of red draw the eye to this table, where elegant red roses and a pretty taxidermied bird with a nest introduce nature to the room.

Right Peace and comfort are the order of the day in this very special library. Classic, leather-bound books and an enormous dictionary resting on the table further enhance the learning that this room inspires.

This is the casual dining area in this home, and as you can see, it is quite spacious and beautiful. A magnificent pine dresser holds many drawers and shelving for silver and china, while an old tub serves as a delightful planter filled with sunny daffodils. Cloches top this table with smaller plant specimens that show off from underneath their protective covering. We also catch a glimpse into a sunroom of incredible French statues. The room has huge banks of windows, and orchids and ferns flourish here.

Right The elegant but relaxed setting welcomes all guests to the dining area of the kitchen.

Below This beautiful statue poses in a graceful stance and adds a softness to the room.

The floor-to-ceiling French doors open onto the garden and, in summer, breezes drift in and about the house, carrying with them the scent of the flowers brought in for entertaining. This is a truly gorgeous, dreamy dining area, complete with a beautifully set table, creamy roses that look like a bride's bouquet, and shimmering crystal candlesticks. The fine aqua and pink china, with monogrammed centers, is a magnificent collection, complemented perfectly by the stemmed crystal goblets, sterling silver place settings, and linen napkins. Heavily scented pink hyacinths planted in silver compotes bring out the pink tones, while blackamoor candelabras cast a gentle light over the buffet. The French chandelier, a prerequisite in a traditional French house, illuminates the dining table, while reflections from the ornate mirror adorned with candles cast an intimate glow.

Previous pages A gorgeous dining room that shimmers in the sunlight with glistening prisms, crystal, and candlesticks, while creating a breathtaking atmosphere.

Left Monogrammed china adds a stunning detail to any dining room.

Right An ornate gilded mirror serves as a tray for the rose bowl centerpiece and candlesticks.

Right Antique mirrors in all shapes and sizes line the magnificent staircase. The statue of the boy, though, is the center of attention, complemented by the huge silver pedestal bowl of white hydrangea pompoms, both displayed on architectural columns.

Below This bedroom is a beautiful color-free sanctuary, containing just the right textures and elements to make it very French and very wonderful.

An incredible staircase and plastered walls welcome you to this home. The landing offers quite the view, with an octagon-shaped window overlooking the grounds, while the peeling frames on the antique French chest create an interesting vignette. Below, an old mirror is quite fabulous, its fading silvering now barely casting a reflection. Green ferns liven up the space and add some softness overall, while the aged architectural columns make a great support for the statue of a boy holding a basket and a fish, and the urn of hydrangeas. At one time, this wonderful, crunchy, layered statue belonged to me. After seeing it here, looking right at home, I think I must have been crazy to part with it.

In any home, a boudoir should speak of romance and subtlety. The surroundings should be soft in color and texture to allow you to drift off to sleep easily. Reflected in the mirror is a collection of aged evening bags hanging dramatically from the door. The gentle curve of the plush couch begs you to relax for a while. The antique mannequin modeling a fur piece makes for an interesting background, along with the long, white plumes that billow from the top of the armoire. Combine those elements with the softness of the layered white fur rug and the velvety down sofa, and you can't help but fall in love with this room.

A BOUDOIR SHOULD SPEAK
OF ROMANCE AND SUBTLETY.

The glistening, gleaming beauty of the chandelier and the crystal on the tea cart is apparent as soon as you enter the dining room. There is an elegant feel to this room but its fanciness is softened with time-worn elements, like the garden statues of baskets of fruit, the antique concrete compote filled with green grapes, heads of lacy cauliflower, and green hydrangeas, and the rusted and peeling tea cart.

By the floor-to-ceiling windows stands a delightful French chair, which acts as the easel for an oil painting. I love its muted, threadbare canvas, which is just a bit tattered. But, as I say throughout this book, things that are imperfect are often the most beautiful. It's like how you can often be more attracted to a charming mutt of a dog than to a prissy pedigree. If something has the right faded, crusted, peeling patina, we know that it has been enjoyed for generations. By whom and where, we don't know, but that is all part of the charm.

Below left Accents of black in the antique hand-painted tole tray and lamp shade give depth to the sparkling display of glass cloches and crystal decanters on the charming rusted tea cart.

Below right The French chair and the faded French oil painting propped up on it are a wonderful mix of faded beauty, and it is their imperfections that make them perfect.

Right This dining area is a perfect example of how a room can come together with the right balance of elegant and time-worn objects.

This pretty, sophisticated floral room is one of ten bathrooms in this mansion. Lighting up the colorful wallpaper of bouquets of huge cabbage roses is a stunning French chandelier. The vase of real roses, in the same hue as those in the wallpaper, bring the paper to life even more. I love the fact that we are welcoming back wallpaper and patterns. A classic pattern never really goes out of style, and by bringing in the right mix of accoutrements you can create a beautiful space, especially in the bathroom. Here, layers of mirrors, lamps, and stunning silver vessels for holding stacks of guest hand towels do just that.

A CLASSIC WALLPAPER
PATTERN NEVER GOES
OUT OF STYLE.

Left A small bath comes to life with gorgeous cabbage roses and wonderful accessories.

Around the next corner is another stunning bath. The chandelier gleams and shines its light down on the aged oil paintings. A bathroom needs all of the special touches that we put in all of the other rooms of the house, but even more. Now to me there is just something about a monogram that says special. It can be any old thing, but once you put a monogram on it, it is transformed into a personalized treasure. There is nothing better than big, fluffy towels outfitted with your own family monogram. I encourage everyone to go out and get some.

Putting this vibrant violet orchid in the mix was an inspired idea. It gives off a stunning pop of color in an otherwise neutral environment. Old oil landscapes placed under the window in a seemingly random spot is different and unexpected. I am always inspired by the unexpected, and I feel that what makes for the best interiors are those little unexpected pieces tossed about throughout your home. These things speak of our individualism, and that is what makes each of our homes so fantastic. We all have our own vision of what our home should look like. That is why it is so important to let your house speak of you and not of Miss Barbara who lives down the street. Miss Barbara does not live in your house everyday. You do.

Above Something as simple as monogrammed towels makes a bathroom more special.

Chapter Five

French Modern

What I would call French modern living is all about a more contemporary, clean style, but not void of interesting objects or the softness that I consider necessary for this look. I grew up with modern. My mother was a genius at being able to mix it with just the right things to make it warm and comfortable, not cold and austere. We would have a mirrored cube as a coffee table layered with glass prisms and acrylic candleholders, but this would be sitting atop a white fur rug, which seemed to soften the cold, hard edges. Lots of texture in low-slung velvet couches and miles of fabric in luxurious drapes helped balance the room. Similarly, these French modern interiors are lush with mohair couches and Venetian mirrors, which come across as chic and urban. Stairs appear to float on air, while banks of windows seem as if you are in the out-of-doors and really make for a breathtaking home. Even though the look is modern, it is still very comfortable and also beautiful.

Left A large expanse of windows allows nature from outdoors to become part of the beauty of the décor.

Being in this room makes you feel as if you are almost in the garden. The magnificent bank of floor-to-ceiling windows allows an unobstructed view of the backyard, with its amazing landscape just beyond the door. The garden is absolutely breathtaking, and you would think that it is set in the middle of a clearing in the woods. In fact, it is off a side street in a busy city, and you would never know. This contemporary look is not short on style, and the neutral palette, along with the soothing sights from outside, make this place an inspiring sanctuary.

CONTEMPORARY STYLING AND A NEUTRAL PALETTE MAKE FOR AN INSPIRING SANCTUARY.

Left A truly gorgeous sunroom that portrays a softness with the all-white color palette, beautiful statuary, and flowering plants.

In this home, one room flows seamlessly into the next, so that you can see into any room from almost anywhere. The magnificent daybed was custom-designed and looks wonderful below the Venetian mirror. The gold tones in the mirror are picked up in the throw tossed on the daybed, and also hinted at in the rug. They're also found in the antique French, leather-bound books displayed next to the antique shell art boxes.

The wall colors seem to flow from beige to golden tones to aqua—all very neutral and natural. The front room is bathed in a gentle aqua shade. This makes a great contrast with the dark casings around the doors and windows, which allow magnificent views onto the pool and surrounding woods. The nondescript fireplace seems to fade quietly into the

Below An antique Scotch dispenser, a crystal rose bowl, and a contemporary chair and couch, covered with a more traditional fabric, give this room a modern look with a traditional twist.

background until it is needed on cold nights. The lamps, works of art in themselves, are fashioned from old architectural fragments. With no handrail or balusters, the remarkable staircase looks as if it is floating on air. In this space, just off the kitchen, is a little sitting area. Another custom-made lamp is found here. I love the chair, with its tufts and marvelously modern shape—surprisingly, very comfy. The modern couch, covered in a more traditional print, with a linen pillow to soften the whole thing up, fits so well here. Although the look is one of casual, urban elegance, where everything seems to flow effortlessly, it was made possible only with thoughtful planning.

Above The den opens up to overlook the living area, so that the home seems to go on forever. The Venetian mirror is a fine backdrop for the daybed.

Left The French shell boxes bring out the gold tones in the antique leather-bound books.

This dining room, near the living area, exudes a comfortable elegance. An enormous old foundry window that has been mirrored reflects the entire space. Galvanized pots of olive trees and a wooden chandelier help make this room a little more rustic than others in the home. The ten-foot-long harvest table is brimming with candles of all shapes and sizes, casting a romantic glow. Antique French chairs decorated with monograms crown the table at either end. Long wood benches provide the rest of the seating. Topiaries add a beautiful shade of green, while the dark olive brown wall color brings a different sort of green tone.

CANDLELIGHT IS THE MASTER OF ATMOSPHERE.

Right Olive trees in pots, a harvest table, and wooden benches help create this rustic take on a modern look.

In this urban French farmhouse, the focal point is the graceful, winding, galvanized staircase, which leads to the galvanized bridge railing up above. This fabulous piece of design allows you to walk on the bridge from one side of the house to the other and look down at all of the goings-on below. An antique zebra rug layering the floor and French antique upholstered chairs create an intimate sitting area. The mercury glass compotes, which make for beautiful planters, and the white French sofas bring a delicate balance to other more masculine elements in the space.

A wine room is conveniently located just off this room, making it easy for guests to replenish their glasses without losing sight of the view.

Above A wine room, with purpose-built storage including display shelves and shuttered cabinets, makes a beautiful addition to this home.

Right The all-white interior is accentuated by the sunny natural landscape beyond the massive doors and windows.

This is an absolutely stunning landscape, from the pool to the water that lies just beyond. Huge trees with graceful limbs stretch out over the yard. The European-style patio extends out over the water, with a French market umbrella, gas lanterns glowing along the exterior trails, and beautiful furniture. These outdoor areas are just as important as the inside of the house and create visitors' first impressions of the home, so it is important to dress up the exterior with beautiful landscaping, lush flower beds, manicured lawns, and sculptured shrubbery. The architecture takes full advantage of the water element here, with an all-glass room that allows one to see across to the water on the far side. Simply gorgeous.

Left and right The beauty of the interior is matched by the gorgeous natural surroundings.

Chapter Six

French Bleu

Many different shades of blue are featured in this chapter, from the pale shade evident in the Asiatic pheasant transferware to the deep cobalt blue of the porcelain vases, planters, and statues. I love them all and for different reasons. Cobalt blue is unsurpassed, and it is amazing how different a plain white room can look when it is added. It is dramatic and powerful, and also a color that I associate with France.

The idea of a cobalt blue bedroom came to me almost like a vision. It stemmed from the antique French toile curtain panels I found at a flea market. They were a bit tattered but I was drawn to their rich color. Over time, I collected just the right bits and pieces to put my vision together. I decided to pair the French *bleu* with elements of silver—the aging silver mercury glass lamp, an ornate French mirror with just the right amount of silvering, and sleek chrome tables. The magic of the combination came together with the rich silk velvet draperies, which hang from a fluted silvered rod and carved finials, and the cobalt silk that is applied to the walls and reflected in the bedding. The vision came to life with the focal point, the aged French doors, which came from France and have different birds displayed in each pane of glass.

Left This bedroom is a stunning display of just how dramatic French *bleu* can be, from the antique toile curtain panels that inspired the decoration to the rich silk velvet draperies and cobalt silk on the walls.

Left Blue makes a lovely accent in this elegant French farmhouse bath.

Below It is amazing how one color can make all the difference and give the eye a focal point in an all-white room. The French shell box and luxurious blue towels are beautiful additional details.

Below right Close up, you can see how beautiful the details truly are. The blue books, the ornate carving on a fabulous antique French sofa, and the delicate coral displayed in a glass compote come together for a gorgeous impact.

I knew immediately that cobalt blue would really add something to this bathroom, so I tweaked and fluffed it with matching towels and a number of fascinating cobalt blue *objets*—the sailor art box from a Paris flea market crowns the entire collection. A wonderful Venetian mirror forms the backdrop. With the addition of blue powder boxes, lipsticks, towels, and such, a truly dramatic statement has been made. Even the "live" element—the rich, bright blue blooms of a hydrangea—looks perfect here.

One wall is fitted with long sconce boxes, an amazing light fixture of sorts, which are enhanced by the light from the many pillar candles. At night, the sconces illuminate the room with a romantic glow, perfect when you're having a soak in the beautiful pedestal tub.

You can really admire the details of the smaller gatherings of *objets* that come together to create this French-inspired space, such as the compote laden with stems of white coral, piled atop antique books. The fabulous tufted French sofa suits the space perfectly. For me, its worn velvet and bits of flaking paint make it all the more wonderful.

The dining room is very French in style, with pale blue walls, beautiful and elaborate toile curtains, and a remarkable and massive table that has been passed down through the generations. The French mirror is unusual—I've never seen anything quite like it before. It is actually a metal harness of a flower garland holding a scalloped mirror inside it.

THIS ROOM IS LAYERED WITH SO MANY GORGEOUS THINGS.

The table centerpiece is a trio of concrete garden cherubs. The flower arrangements with purple orchids are a lovely addition. From bright violet to periwinkle to iris blue, I love the color combinations in this room. I searched high and low to find just the right shades of purple and blue for the collection of compotes and bowls. My obsession with transferware has led to many colors and combinations for entertaining. This table lends itself to the partnering of plum transferware— always brought out on Christmas Eve—with pale blue Asiatic pheasant, which is my favorite. Antique ribbons and hat flowers make pretty decorations for the chairs.

Left The room is set off by the background color of pale French blue, which appears in the wall color and the toile panels, highlighting the blue transferware. The table setting is a successful mix of violet and different shades of blue, with plum transferware, making a fresh, new color combination.

This could be a patio in France or a courtyard in New Orleans, containing all of the architectural elements to transport you to another world. Old concrete fountains and the soothing sound of trickling water, urns, and statuary are all here, as well as peeling posts with hanging lanterns that light up the space at night.

The French *bleu* elements burst forth in the wonderful tabletop display of porcelain. Taking center stage, though, are the crusted, peeling, outdoor chairs. The graceful curve of the back and legs gives off a femininity that is just as beautiful inside as outdoors. Plants are everywhere, with ferns, palms, and budding white hydrangeas adding so much to the overall color here. Concrete statuary is dotted around the patio, interspersed with all sorts of blue porcelain.

Right A courtyard patio becomes even more inviting with the blue and white porcelain adding some delicate color to this paradise.

Below The ornate table and chairs have a gentle curved shape, which I love. Graceful and feminine, they add a romantic element, whether they're used inside or out. They look gorgeous with the blue and white porcelain planters and vases.

Chapter Seven

Display

We all personalize our homes through display, surrounding ourselves with objects that we treasure, and much can be learned about our personalities from them.

Inspiration for our displays can come from anywhere, from the delicate pink of a tattered and worn pair of ballet shoes to a painting picked up at a Paris flea market. Just by looking at the interiors in this book, you can see how important display is to their overall appeal. I love to display artwork on my walls. As I have said elsewhere, the monetary value of the art is irrelevant. What matters is that I feel a connection with the piece and it draws me in. The displays that you create should reflect your passions. These could be different photographs that you have taken during your travels. Framed and made into a wall collage, they bring treasured memories flooding back. Elements from nature, such as bug collections, shells, even old book plates of mushrooms, can make wonderful collections throughout your home. Glass cloches make the perfect display cases.

Left This French country-style display reveals an idiosyncratic passion for cows and blue Spode dishes. A pine Welsh dresser makes a beautiful backdrop and enhances the display even further.

After all my planning and collecting to achieve the perfect look, my favorite part of this business is being able to see my finished creations. My friend and I collaborated and collected to come up with this eye-catching garden and nature display using items from her store. A crumbling statue is the centerpiece, with an ancient garden fence, still entwined with vines, forming the backdrop. Nature themes always make for intriguing displays, and this table is piled high with *objets* taken from the natural world. Either side of the display are old French store doors with wonderful French writing.

Displays in a store window need to be awe-inspiring—each vignette has to be studied closely and for a good length of time before every part of it can be fully appreciated. Such extravagant displays would be over the top in the home but they are a fruitful source of inspiration, encouraging you to achieve a similar effect but on a smaller scale.

Left An eclectic mix of all sorts of discoveries from nature.

Right The old statuary is the centerpiece of this garden and nature display.

Displays can be made up of so many things, from a substantial piece of antique furniture to some simple utilitarian supplies arranged in an artful way. An incredibly ornate table discovered at a Paris flea market becomes the focus of this display when placed on an entry landing and enhanced with a collection of gorgeous antique frames.

Even the most functional of rooms deserve a display of some kind. In this kitchen, the palest of pink flowers are the perfect finishing touch. Resting atop a pale blue Asiatic Pheasant china pedestal, kitchen essentials such as dish soap have been repackaged to become objects worthy of display, while the scented candle not only freshens the air but is pretty in its own right. Mundane items elsewhere can also be transformed to become objects of beauty, such as mouthwash repackaged in a crystal decanter.

Right An ornate French table makes quite a statement displayed on this landing.

Below A captivating display of both function and beauty.

This rolling cart makes for a great coffee table display. The old French cloche, which once covered seedlings in the garden, is now fogged from years of weathering, making it even more desirable. The red coral is stunning and adds a splash of color to an otherwise neutral room. I do so enjoy the way in which many things that seem insignificant when alone can be brought together for an amazing display.

Below A coffee table cart is decorated with an interesting assortment of *objets trouvés*.

Over the years, I have collected some beautiful pieces of French shell art, mostly from Parisian flea markets and often decorated with French writing. Older examples are, sadly, quite hard to find now. Also known as sailor valentines, as sailors would have created them for their loved ones back home, shell art comes in different forms, such as boxes and small pictures, and makes a beautiful addition to any space.

Below These French shell boxes are beautiful works of art from the past.

An antique French mirror tops off this faux mantel beautifully. A teardrop chandelier reflects in the mirror and blends with the other French elements, including a tufted chair and a gorgeous statue of a woman.

A glorious example of the natural world—an abandoned robin's nest, complete with tiny blue eggs—was discovered just outside the front door. Brought inside and placed under an antique glass cloche atop a cake pedestal, it has become an unusual display piece. The cloche allows the intricate nest to be viewed at close quarters while also protecting it.

Left Trophy cups serve as vases on this antique mantel.

Right An abandoned nest has been placed under a glass cloche to create an unusual and pretty display.

In these two beautiful spaces—a bathroom and a sunroom—it is easy to see how important "live" elements are in a display. The surround of a huge garden tub is often an ignored space, but the display here shows how truly amazing it can be. A crusted French garden urn, planted with a green lacy fern, and a French statue of a woman, who looks as if she could be filling the tub with water, conspire to make this bath a place where you would want to linger. The collection of brown transferware is the perfect backdrop.

In the breathtaking sunroom, the white-painted cabinet serves as the base for many inspiring display pieces, but the focus is undeniably the gorgeous lacy fern, surrounded by aged concrete statuary, mercury glass candlesticks, and other plants.

Left A normally unused bathtub surround makes an incredible display area.

Right The vibrant greenery brings this sunroom to life.

In the sunroom, the amazing, ornately decorated window, which you can imagine was salvaged from a French building of some distinction, catches the eye immediately. Equally impressive is the aged religious statue set on the base of a fountain, which makes for a fitting pedestal. The light, as it streams into the room, only seems to add to the grandeur of the statue. Religious pieces are popular in French interiors, although the larger statues are often difficult to find. Graceful and delicate white blooms and greenery enclose the space, making it an intimate and peaceful retreat.

The small, flaking statue of the Madonna and Child, with a backdrop of a mirror framed with shells, sits on a shelf as the centerpiece of another display. Like the large statue, it has been given the perfect setting.

Left A small, time-worn statue of the Madonna and Child is the eye-catching feature of this shelf display.

Right Standing in the base of a stone fountain, this piece of religious statuary makes for an arresting display.

Index

Acknowledgments

First and foremost, I would like to thank each one of you for buying a copy of this book. For me, each book is a labor of love. I put much of myself into each word and photograph and do my best to try and make it a book that you will be proud to own. So, from me to you, thank you.

Next, I would like to thank everyone at CICO Books who made this happen. Thanks to David Peters, Cindy Richards, Gillian Haslam, and the entire team. To them I owe much gratitude.

Where, oh where would I be without such fabulous photography? Here's to my talented and diplomatic photographer, Mr Keith Scott Morton, who I was fortunate enough to work with... you are truly a legend. I must give a shout out to your wife Chris and daughter Natasha, who were stuck in NYC, but who did get a pretty fabulous pair of cowboy boots out of the deal. We will not forget the trials, tribulations, and sometimes close quarters that brought us close together, and the back roads quest for the best bar-b-que. It was my honor to work with you.

To Eric Richards... the other part of the photography genius who worked on the book and who was quite the gentleman, fixing the things that I could not reach, carrying the heavy stuff once the shoot was over, and who could not wait to get back to the slopes in Vermont.

To my family: Joe, Victoria, Alex, Nicholas, and not to forget Mom (Charlotte) and Dad (Chuck)... When they say it takes a village, they were not kidding. Thanks for waiting dinner, waiting while I was gone for extended periods, putting up with my ridiculous schedule, and helping make sure that the kids were where they needed to be and eating right, when I couldn't. Family is what it is all about and I love you all. It just would not be family without mentioning my Jack (the big black lab), who is always out to greet me at the end of the road when he hears me coming, and Princess and Teddy, who meet me at the door... always a great welcome back.

To Joe: a wonderful husband and supporter and the other half of my life and my business. I love you and could not do what I do, without you.

To Victoria: one smart and creative cookie... not to mention beautiful inside and out.

To Alex: to one who is not only beautiful and smart, but able to be both the photographer and the model at the same time... that's talent.

To Nick: to the only 13-year-old that I know who can do anything... trim trees, drive a tractor, also quite the photographer, trumpet player, fisherman, and four-wheelin' young man. I don't know what I would do without your help... I love your passion, your diversity, and growing up with all of these women means that you will make someone a fabulous husband, someday.

To Charlotte: you have always been an inspiration to all who know you, in all aspects of life, not just decorating, which is why you are so remarkable. XOXO

To Dad: the rock of the entire family. Much love to you.

To my friends: Kathy and Donny Gross, who offered me shelter while I had to be roaming about on my travels. You are both creative souls and if you cannot find the cool stuff, you make it. You know the good stuff in life and live it to the fullest. Much love to you both.

To my talented friend Gina Tomelleri and her husband, Alan, whose fabulous store vignette can be found in the Display chapter of the book. While visiting Gina's store, as I often do, we collaborated on some great displays and became very inspired. It is great to have people in your life who offer support and even better, when you can offer each other great inspiration. The dreamers of the world unite, my friend. Keep living your passion and loving what you do. I am proud to call you my friend.

I would like to thank each and every one of my friends and clients who graciously opened up their homes to be a part of the book. I am very rich in friendships and have a wonderful, diverse group of creative, caring souls. I am blessed to get to live my passion and have met some very talented people along my journey through life. Here's to the good stuff, my friends!

Each one of these houses is as diverse as the homeowner and I appreciate all of you who opened your doors to all of us.

To Janet Weibe: to someone who has the pleasure of spending so much time in France and who has extraordinary taste. Thanks for making the introductions between Charyl and myself... you are a great colleague and friend.

To Charyl Coleman: you are one talented person. We actually were introduced through mutual friends, and when Charyl mentioned that she had done the interiors at the Havana hotel in San Antonio when they had their redo some years back, I told her, "You had me at Havana." It was magnificent, and I was able to coerce Charyl into lending some of her clients' interiors as a part of the book and I am all the better for it. She opened up the doors to some of her clients who were Mrs. Susan Walker and Bea Sanger. I appreciate the glimpses into their lovely décor and for taking the time out of their busy schedules to be a part of this work.

To Angie and Mike Cavalier: your house is a gloriously neutral palette with a bathroom to die for. Thanks for letting us in and rearranging your world and your schedule to accommodate us. It looks beautiful in print and I am glad that we got to share this opportunity.

To Sheila and Eric Langford: Sheila, I appreciate you letting us in to rearrange and discombobulate all of your surroundings, not to mention the tasty spread that you so effortlessly seemed to put together for me and my hungry photography team. The photographs were marvelous and what a house to work in. Truly awe-inspiring, my friend.

To Carla and Rob Cline: I have to admit, before doing this shoot, I was a bit afraid of Rob Cline. Every time Carla was on a shopping adventure and spending money, it seemed to always be with me... gee, imagine that. I would never want Carla to write a check or Rob would be upset with me, not her, for not being able to resist that perfect little thing, like the lake house that she bought him as a birthday surprise. You see, the truth is, she just needed another place to furnish. Here's to one of the kindest hearts I know, and for keeping my daughter's scholarship pages filled with your co-chaired philanthropy projects, and to her husband Rob, who I now know and love... wish he could say the same. He's still grumbling about that wonderful, ripped and dilapidated chair. To a beautiful house filled with beautiful people.

To Michelle and Joel Bruner: Michelle is a designer and a client of mine who was previously with Ralph Lauren Home Collection. I was lucky enough to talk her into being a part of the book and she was quite insecure about the whole project, but has one of the most beautiful houses that I have ever seen. I keep telling her, it is not the size but the content. She has mastered the art of design and I walked in and did very little, as it was photo-worthy when I arrived. Her skills from the Ralph Lauren store shined through and it was quite a reward for me to have someone so talented in my book. Her husband Joel was quite the good sport with all of the round-the-clock work involved and her daughter Emma was great help and her room an inspiration. Thanks to all of you!

To Lauren and Ned Ross: beautiful. Your house is filled with warmth and beauty and, of course, Lauren's amazing talent. This is not the first book that Lauren has been a part of and it looked like our scheduling would not work out until the very end... so glad it did. I love your love of the details and it shows in the remarkable photos. Your house is as feminine and beautiful as you are and I am proud to have your home as a part of my project. Thanks, Lauren.

To Jacqueline and Steve: what can I say about Jacqueline... she is one of the most outgoing, hardworking, talented people that I know, who believes, as I do, in living life to the fullest. We are two strong-willed, hard-headed women, who try to fit as much in a day as possible before you crash into the bed at night. She has many properties, in the U.S. and abroad, and has traveled the world and experienced life. Her husband Steve is as supportive as they come, and together they create a beautiful home for living and entertaining wherever home may be at the time. Jacqueline is not one who is short on words and gave me some pearls of wisdom to live by from her grandmother, "One life well lived is sufficient"—Olive Dalton. Another famous quote from Jacqueline's mother, Mrs. Marilyn Kahanec, was, "We should all be more like toothpaste and just merely ooze into the day." These are both quotes to live by. Here's to more Paris living and of course, San Miguel.

I would also like to thank all of the creative people that I work with on a daily basis... to Paul and his creative team who keep my website humming... www.carolynwestbrookhome.com.

To Jane: who has stuck with me through thick and thin... Thanks to you.

And to my business, Carolyn Westbrook Home, which is much like my child and which Joe and I have worked so hard to grow and prosper over the years, from nothing into fruition. It has been quite a ride, but I am very fortunate that I live my passion.

A book is such a collaboration and there are many people involved and working hard to help my dream come to life. Thanks to everyone that was a part and a support, and again to all of you for reading my words and looking at the photos here.

XOXO Carolyn

Keep up-to-date with my book signings, products, and other events by visiting my website: www.carolynwestbrookhome.com